Instagram

Kevin Systrom
and Mike Krieger

INTERNET BIOGRAPHIES™

Instagram
Kevin Systrom
and Mike Krieger

KRISTEN RAJCZAK

ROSEN PUBLISHING®

New York

Published in 2015 by The Rosen Publishing Group, Inc.
29 East 21st Street, New York, NY 10010

Library of Congress Cataloging-in-Publication Data

Rajczak, Kristen, author.
Instagram: Kevin Systrom and Mike Krieger/Kristen Rajczak.—First
edition.
    pages cm.—(Internet biographies)
Includes bibliographical references and index.
ISBN 978-1-4777-7917-0 (library bound: alk. paper)
1. Systrom, Kevin, 1983—Juvenile literature. 2. Krieger, Mike,
1986—Juvenile literature. 3. Instagram (Firm—Biography—
Juvenile literature. 4. Image files—Juvenile literature. 5. Computer
file sharing—Juvenile literature. 6. Software engineering—
Biography—Juvenile literature. I. Title.
TR267.5.I57R35 2015
770.285530922—dc23

                                        2014012317

Manufactured in the United States of America

Contents

INTRODUCTION

In July 2011, Justin Bieber signed up for Instagram. He was just months off of the release of his biopic–concert movie *Justin Bieber: Never Say Never.* The behind-the-scenes film was a huge hit with his ravenous tween fan base, so joining the social media network that allowed everyday people into the daily lives of celebrities was a no-brainer opportunity. As of March 2014, he'd posted almost 1,300 times. Bieber, along with rapper Snoop Dogg, reality TV personality Kim Kardashian, and singer Rihanna, has embraced the photo-sharing app as another way to connect with fans, and all four celebrities boast millions of Instagram followers to prove it. The explosion of celebrities on Instagram truly shows the app's broad reach and genius ability to keep users engaged—with themselves, each other, and their favorite famous names.

Cofounders Kevin Systrom and Mike Krieger drew on the knowledge and connections they gained as Stanford University students when they started working on the photo-sharing app that would become Instagram. They share a wealth of technology experience, having collectively worked for some of the biggest names in the

Instagram has become a great way for celebrities, such as Justin Bieber, to connect with their fans.

tech world—Google, Odeo (which became Twitter), and Microsoft included. But it's the fusion of their individual passions that's truly at the heart of Instagram. Systrom has been interested in photography since high school, and Krieger has long studied the improvement of user interface. These, blended with their particular talent for perceiving the needs of social media users, have allowed them to successfully navigate the development, launch, and sale of Instagram. They're young, brilliant, and today remain dedicated to Instagram's development. Even under the umbrella of another social media giant—Facebook— Systrom and Krieger are stalwart believers in their ultimately good-hearted mission: "To capture and share the world's moments." They want the photos shared on Instagram to reflect the best of the world around us, and perhaps a better world only seen from behind a camera lens—or a sepia-toned filter.

From "selfie" culture to ever-present food photography, Instagram has changed the way social media users share their pictures. But Instagram hasn't affected only the *way* photos are shared, though the app's connectivity to Twitter, Facebook, Flickr, and Foursquare has vastly improved the ease of photo sharing. Instagram and its myriad filters have changed *what's* being shared. While there are plenty of selfies still popping up on the app's feed, more people are taking the time to look at the world around them through the fresh perspective of the Hefe or Lomo-fi filter—and making their flower pots, utensils, and streets look more glamorous and nostalgic. In the fast-moving tech world, it may be too soon to laud their accomplishments with Instagram, but so far, Krieger and Systrom have helped users make good on their vision.

How did Systrom and Krieger become such successful entrepreneurs long before either turned thirty? Trial and error, persistence, observation, and perhaps a little luck played into the story of Kevin Systrom, Mike Krieger, and their innovative Instagram.

CHAPTER 1

Kevin Systrom: Computer Whiz Kid, Passionate Photographer

Kevin Systrom was born December 30, 1983, to Doug and Diane Systrom. He grew up in Holliston, a suburb of Boston, Massachusetts. Systrom's interest in technology started early. By age twelve, he was using AOL (America Online) to play pranks on his friends, controlling their cursors or kicking them offline. In high school, Systrom was excused from taking a foreign language class to take more computer science classes. He was exposed to the startup business mentality as a child. His mother, Diane, began working in marketing for Monster.com soon after the website's launch. It was clear that business was in his blood when Systrom expressed an interest in it to a local newspaper in 2002. The Middlesex School alumni magazine reported Systrom had said he wanted to "come up with an idea that is unique and that people come away from and say, 'That was fun.'"

Of course, computers and business weren't the only things on Systrom's teenage mind. At Holliston High

School, Systrom ran cross-country, even earning the Rookie of the Year award his first year on the team as an eighth grader. Two years later, when Systrom transferred to the Middlesex School—a boarding school in nearby Concord, Massachusetts—he became known for his love of photography. While a student at Middlesex, Systrom did graphic design for the school's newspapers and founded the school's radio station. With such an obviously innovative spirit, it's no surprise that he won the Frederick Winsor Book Prize for academic initiative and the first Lawrence Terry Book Prize for distinguished contributions to the life of the school.

STARTING AT STANFORD

After graduating from high school in 2002, Systrom enrolled at Stanford University in Stanford, California. He wanted to study computer science. However, Systrom tried to take an advanced programming class his first semester at Stanford—and was barely able to get a B, even though he was working forty hours a week on just that class. "I looked around and saw so many fantastically smart folks in that class and decided I was better off majoring in something like business," Systrom wrote on the question-and-answer website Quora.com. Systrom ended up majoring in management science and engineering.

Systrom's years at Stanford would prove to be the most transformative of his life. He joined the Sigma Nu fraternity

When Kevin Systrom enrolled in Stanford University, he was walking in the footsteps of many other tech-company wizards, including Brian Acton, the cofounder of WhatsApp, and David Filo, the cofounder of Yahoo!

and worked on building a few games and websites, including a short stint running Stanford's version of Craigslist. He also built a website called PhotoBox for his fraternity to post pictures from parties.

Systrom's college classmates told the *New York Times* that his photography and design skills were clear in his visually stunning class presentations. As a junior, he took this passion even further. Systrom studied abroad in Florence, Italy. Instead of computers or engineering, Systrom decided to focus on photography while there. He packed his Nikon SLR, or single-lens reflex camera, a type of camera he'd been using since attending the Middlesex School. But while in Florence, a teacher handed Systrom a plastic Holga, a camera made in Hong Kong, China, that took square photographs. The soft focus and light distortions he was able to achieve with the Holga changed how Systrom looked at his photographs in a way that would come back years later.

Systrom's time studying photography in Italy taught him to see the world around him in a new way.

Systrom applied to the competitive Mayfield Fellows Program while he was still in

What's an App?

When Kevin Systrom was in college at Stanford, apps weren't quite the phenomenon they are today. However, much of the web building he did as an undergraduate student later translated into this new world of programming.

"App" is short for "application." An application is a piece of computer software that allows a user to perform a task. The software can be on a desktop computer or a mobile device, though the shortening of the word "application" to "app" most often refers to mobile applications in everyday speech. The software programs used on a computer are commonly called desktop applications. Some desktop applications might include word-processing programs, such as Microsoft Word, that allow you to create text documents. Web browsers, including Firefox, Safari, and Google Chrome, are also applications. iTunes and other media players, as well as games, can be desktop applications, too.

The apps that are discussed here refer to the apps users purchase from app stores, such as Google Play or the Apple App Store. Apps are often free, or if not, cost only a few dollars to download. Some apps aim to make the tasks users do on their mobile devices simpler or better somehow, like organizing browser bookmarks. Others are just for fun! As more people begin to use smartphones and tablets, mobile apps have become big business. Apple reported that its App Store made $10 billion in profits in 2013. An article in *Forbes* included some incredible stats about the app market:

- Google products have about 900 million mobile users, followed by Apple with 600 million users, and Microsoft with about 12 million.

- Apple has about 1.25 million apps available in the App Store, which account for about 50 billion downloads.

- Google has about 150,000 app developers who have created more than 800,000 apps.

- Microsoft reported its average user downloads 54 apps.

The present business models bring more profit to these big companies selling the apps than those creating them. But with market growth that shows no sign of slowing, there are still opportunities for the next big app hit.

Italy. He was accepted and began the nine-month program when he returned to Stanford.

EMERGING ENTREPRENEUR

Through the Mayfield Fellows Program, Systrom earned a summer internship at a podcast company called Odeo. Odeo would later morph into the microblogging site Twitter. Jack Dorsey, the man Systrom sat next to at Odeo, would be the one to do it in early 2006. Odeo was Systrom's first time working at a startup. It gave him a taste of the pace and drive needed to make a new company work.

Jack Dorsey founded both Twitter and the online payment company Square.

Startup Boot Camp

In 2005, Systrom entered the Mayfield Fellows Program. It combines both classes and work experiences, and accepts only twelve students each year. Systrom described it to *Forbes* as "a crash-course business school for startups." The Mayfield Fellows Program website calls the program a way for students to "develop a theoretical and practical understanding of the techniques for growing technology companies." Students in the fellowship program make connections with actual startup companies around San Francisco, as well as venture capitalists. "Venture capital" refers to the funds gathered to start a business, and a venture capitalist is someone who provides this funding.

While a Mayfield Fellow, Systrom made important connections that he'd call on after graduating from Stanford. Tina Seelig, the coordinator of the Mayfield Fellowship Program, told *Forbes* that Systrom was a standout among the young entrepreneurs in the program: "It was in his nature to be looking at the world through the lens of 'Where's the opportunity here?'"

The Mayfield Fellows Program is only available to Stanford students, though they can be from any academic subject area. It includes classes, an

(continued on the next page)

(continued from the previous page)

internship, networking, and mentorship. To apply, students must complete an online form, followed by submission of a résumé, personal statement, unofficial transcript, and a list of recommenders, as well as two letters of recommendation. These applications are due at the beginning of February each year. From those who apply, a group is called for interviews. At the beginning of March, the final dozen students are selected.

On Quora.com, Systrom wrote, "It turns out that no undergrad class prepares you to start a startup—you learn most of it as you do it." Fortunately for him, as a Mayfield Fellow, he had practical experiences to draw on, as well as classes.

He told the *LA Times*, "That first day, I decided I wanted to be an entrepreneur."

During his last semesters in college, Systrom earned invaluable hands-on experience. But had one dinner ended differently, he wouldn't have finished at Stanford at all. Systrom had met Facebook founder Mark Zuckerberg at a party one night. Then, the summer before Systrom started his senior year, Zuckerberg took Systrom out to dinner and asked him to drop out of Stanford to join the Facebook team. Zuckerberg wanted Systrom to work on Facebook's new photo feature for him. Systrom said no and began his final year at Stanford, graduating in 2006. After graduation, Systrom took a job working at Google, though he had received a more lucrative offer from Microsoft. He first worked writing marketing materials for Gmail and Google Calendar, but told *Forbes* he found the job boring after a while. Systrom then worked in corporate development at Google and learned how technology business deals, including acquisitions, were done behind the scenes. After less than three years, Systrom left Google.

His next stop was NextStop, a startup website founded by some of his coworkers at Google. The site was for travel recommendations, and Systrom truly started the next phase of his career there. He worked in marketing for Next-Stop, but at night began to play with new, simple ideas that taught him the basics of programming. On Quora.com, Systrom went as far as to say he went from "a hobbyist to being able to write code that would go into production." His programming skills, business sense, and creativity were quickly weaving together with each new venture.

CHAPTER 2

Mike Krieger and the User Experience

Mike Krieger was born March 4, 1986, in São Paolo, Brazil. Technology, engineering, and the way people interact with computers began to interest him in his teens.

As a high school student, Krieger worked in a program after school teaching computer skills to maintenance workers at his school. The experience was eye opening. Though Krieger was old enough to have grown up using computers and other technology, these workers were frustrated with actions as simple as double-clicking a mouse. Fittingly, Krieger later told *GQ* that his favorite movie in high school was *Lost in Translation*. The movie stars Scarlett Johansson and Bill Murray as an unlikely pair who meet while traveling in Toyko, Japan. In part, the movie highlights the language and cultural barrier between the travelers and the people they meet in Japan. The language barriers in the movie can be easily compared to the technology barriers Krieger saw the

São Paulo is the largest city in the Southern Hemisphere. Today, the city has a population greater than ten million and a metro-area population of about nineteen million!

older maintenance workers encounter in the after-school program. The experience not only made him realize the connection—and frequent disconnection—between technology and users, but it also made him question these interactions. "Why do you click on things once on the web but twice on your desktop?" Krieger was quoted asking in a post by Ellis Hamburger on TheVerge.com. "I knew I was interested in making that better for people and studying how we can take the goal of what the interface is and make that work for people."

WELCOME TO THE UNITED STATES!

The seeds of improving interface were already planted when Krieger arrived at Stanford University in 2004. He chose symbolic systems as his major, a mixture of computer science, psychology, and linguistics. The program fit his interests and had some impressive graduates, including Yahoo! CEO Marissa Mayer (1997) and the cofounder of LinkedIn, Reid Hoffman (1990). Krieger wrote on the White House Blog (WhiteHouse.gov) that as a student at Stanford, he was very "inspired" by nearby startups and Silicon Valley business leaders. Like Systrom, he was accepted to the Mayfield Fellows Program and had great access to many mentors in the field.

THE NEVER-ENDING PROCESS

When Krieger moved to the United States to attend Stanford in 2004, he would have been considered an international student. This means applying to school would have been more difficult and included several more steps for him than an American citizen applying to schools around the United States. College Board International suggests international students start looking into the process two years before they would begin classes. International applicants still have to take whatever standardized tests the college or university requires, such as the SAT or ACT. Often they also have to take an exam proving proficiency in English, such as

Marissa Mayer started as CEO of Yahoo! in 2012 after working for Google for thirteen years. According to *Forbes*, she spent more than $100 million on acquisitions in 2013.

the TOEFL (Test of English as a Foreign Language), which tests English reading, writing, speaking, and listening in an academic setting. Even if an international student does well on these and has a strong overall application, *US News & World Report* stated that international students only make up about 10 percent of most college classes, so the odds of getting into a competitive school like Stanford are much less. After being accepted to a college or university in the United States, an international student must then receive an F-1, or student, visa.

Immigrant Entrepreneurs

In a post on the White House Blog in 2012, Krieger wrote about meeting the president and the first lady, the chief technology officer of the United States, and others to speak about encouraging entrepreneurship among immigrants. As an immigrant entrepreneur himself, Krieger wrote that he was pleased to see better opportunities for foreign-born students in the United States, particularly in the science, technology, engineering, and math fields. He had hope that future U.S. immigration policies would allow them the opportunity to start the businesses they want to.

Krieger isn't the only one thinking about the talents immigrant entrepreneurs can bring to the United States and the opportunities the country can help them pursue. In a post on *Forbes*'s Techonomy blog, Yatin Mundkur highlights the "fertile" environment of innovation in the United States. "It's hard to question the necessity of tapping the best pool of talent—homegrown and foreign—to maintain our leadership as innovators," Mundkur wrote. Edward Alden wrote on the Council on Foreign Relations Renewing America blog that there's a great history of entrepreneurship among U.S. immigrants, but that they could be better used and supported as businesspeople in the United States. He specifically calls out Latinos, the fastest-growing immigrant group in the United States, as a big potential source of entrepreneurship.

Krieger is just one example of the entrepreneurial spirit brought to the United States by smart, talented immigrants. He would likely agree with Mundkur that bringing together people and ideas from around the world can only make companies stronger. "No country has nurtured innovation better than the United States, in large part due to our ability to attract the best minds in science and engineering from around the world," Mundkur wrote. "Diversity is one of our country's greatest strengths."

For Krieger and others who want to stay in the United States after graduation, this isn't the end of the paperwork. Krieger was able to work for a year on his student visa but then had to apply for an H-1B visa, which gives skilled immigrants permission to work within U.S. borders. According to U.S. Citizenship and Immigration Services (USCIS), there are several requirements one needs to meet to be granted an H-1B visa, including that the job "must qualify as a specialty occupation" and it must be in the field you studied. Krieger would have had to prove that he had a special set of skills and that he had an employer willing to pay him for his work. An additional hurdle H-1B visa applicants must overcome is the limited number of these visas available each year—only sixty-five thousand may be granted. Fortunately, when Krieger applied, a visa was available for him.

Krieger's efforts to stay in the United States didn't end there. He applied for a green card at the beginning of 2012. A green card is the documentation proving someone is allowed to live and work in the United States. The USCIS website lists the many ways to apply for a green card, including through a job. It can be through a job offer or an investment, or if a person works a specific kind of job. Immigrants can also file for a green card through "self petition," or file on behalf of themselves. One group of immigrants that can apply for green cards in this way are those with "extraordinary ability in the sciences, arts, education, business, or athletics." Sometimes they're called "Aliens of Extraordinary Ability"! However an immigrant files for his or her green card, there's a lot of information the government needs—photos, medical history, and biographical facts. Green cards are good for ten years, and then they need to be renewed.

Mike Krieger was known as a talented software engineer, and his skills only grew as he gained experience.

SCHOOL AND BEYOND

Krieger was a leader in his department at Stanford. He advised prospective and current students about the symbolic systems program. For almost all his years at Stanford, Krieger served as a tutor to students making oral presentations, even visiting classes to give tips on oral communications. In addition, he interned at Microsoft from June to September 2006. There, he worked on PowerPoint, OfficeArt, and photo features. The next year, Krieger was an intern with Foxmarks, Inc., later called Xmarks, a company that produced add-ons to web browsers.

When Krieger graduated in 2008, he had earned both a bachelor's and a master's degree in symbolic systems. According to the Instagram website, his master's thesis was on "how user interfaces can better support collaboration on a large scale"—a topic that seemed years in the making for Krieger. From there, he took his skills to Meebo, an instant messaging service, where he worked as a user experience designer and engineer. He met Meebo's founders while working there and began to observe how to run a small company.

CHAPTER 3

Checking In and Checking Out

In 2009, suddenly social network users could find out where their friends were at all times. "Checking in" with a new app called Foursquare became all the rage. Checking in refers to a user adding, or allowing the addition of, his or her location on a social media site or online post. By checking in to a location, users could see who else was at a location, even people they didn't know. By the spring of 2010, Facebook began working on location features as well, adding their "Places" feature in August of that year. Places allowed users not only to check in but also link to—or tag—the friends with them.

THE FIRST IDEA

While working at NextStop, Kevin Systrom had an idea for an app that used location services and felt he finally had the skills to tackle it. He wanted to build an app with a check-in feature. It would be like Foursquare, but with a

Where Are You?

Today, location services are available through just about every social media network, not just Foursquare. From Twitter and Facebook to Instagram, you can check in to restaurants, sporting events, movie theaters, and more. Additionally, the mobile app version of mapping tools, such as Google Maps, can pinpoint your location for easy direction. Recommendation sites Yelp and UrbanSpoon also use location services to guide users to establishments in their desired area.

Sometimes a user inputs his or her location when checking in or using an app. Other times, the app uses data from the cellular network, Wi-Fi, or Global Positioning System (GPS) capabilities of a mobile device to supply the location. Assigning location information gathered from a mobile device to a photo, status update, or other online post is called geotagging. As of January 2014, Foursquare has used this technology to create a community of more than forty-five million users checking in over five billion times, according to the Foursquare website.

The benefits of location services are many. If you're lost, simply input the address of where you'd like to go into your mapping app and find your way. If you need a quick meal, simply search for the closest restaurants. Location services are popular, too. The Pew Research Center reported that of the 91 percent of adult Americans who owned a cell phone in 2013, 49 percent used it to "get directions, recommendations, or other location-based information." Only about 8 percent used their phones to "'check in' or share [their] location." This lower percentage could have been due to privacy concerns. Microsoft.com lists one risk of using location services as quite frightening: "Services, such as Foursquare, that track your location can be used for criminal purposes—for spying, stalking or theft... there is no limit to who might know where you are and when you're not at home."

In 2011, Nielsen reported that 52 percent of male and 59 percent of female mobile app users were concerned about the privacy of checking in. The report predicted that the more familiar users are with location services, the more comfortable with them they would become.

As technology continues to improve, the better location services will get. Pay attention to the privacy settings on your apps and take a moment to think if choosing to check in is a smart idea before you do so.

According to Foursquare's website, over 1.7 million businesses use Foursquare's Merchant Platform. This lets businesses take control of their name on Foursquare and see what customers are saying.

game aspect to it, stemming from the popularity of a game called *Mafia Wars* by software developer Zynga. He called the app Burbn, a tribute to his favorite drink, bourbon. He started working on the weekends, building the prototype in HTML5, and letting his friends try it out.

In January 2010, Systrom was at a party hosted by a startup called Hunch, along with many venture capitalists. He met Steve Anderson, the founder of Baseline Ventures and a Twitter investor. Right there, Systrom brought up the Burbn prototype on his iPhone and showed it to Anderson.

All About HTML

"HTML" stands for "HyperText Markup Language." Website addresses often end in .html. That's because HTML is the code used to create the World Wide Web, consisting of text written in a specific way to produce the content of a website. Scientist Tim Berners-Lee first introduced it in 1990. HTML 5 is the fifth version of the markup language. While HTML can describe the font and color of text or shapes on a website, it wasn't originally designed to do so. These additions can make the code very long and difficult to comb through for maintenance. To solve this problem, the World Wide Web Consortium (W3C) created CSS, or Cascading Style Sheets. CSS is a separate text file—or style sheet—from a website's HTML code. It's written into the HTML document to refer to a style sheet for a website's look and format, including color and font.

When Kevin Systrom showed his app to investor Steve Anderson, Anderson was pleased to see that it had been written in HTML5, what Steve Bertoni of *Forbes* called the "it" code of the time. It remains the industry standard today. One reason HTML5 is desirable to web developers is that it's supported by the most current browsers, making development

(continued on the next page)

(continued from the previous page)

time of products written in HTML5 faster. It also goes hand in hand with CSS3, the latest version of CSS. CSS3 uses fewer lines of code to do more than its predecessors, reducing the number of files needed for a product.

The top reason Anderson—and other developers and investors—would have been pleased with the use of HTML5 in Burbn is the code's ability to support both sites viewed on a desktop computer and a mobile device. At a time when the mobile market was growing exponentially, mobile-friendly code would have been a significant asset to a product. What's even more remarkable is that Systrom was a mostly self-taught programmer. He'd had experience with some coding during high school and college, but it was through hard work on his own time that he was able to gain enough experience to code successfully in HTML5 and CSS3.

Anderson saw potential in the idea. He later recalled seeing the app to writers of the *New York Times*, "We knew mobile was going to be important, and we knew that there was an opportunity to create compelling experiences for

To those who don't know CSS or HTML, the text can look like a foreign language. Yet it's the basis for what everyone does on the Internet.

mobile devices, but we didn't know a heck of a lot more than that." After meeting with Systrom again, Anderson invested $250,000 in Burbn. With that, Systrom decided to leave NextStop after just over a year and start a company around developing Burbn. Investors from Andreessen Horowitz, who also met Systrom at the party, would contribute another $250,000 soon after. Interestingly, Andreessen Horowitz later invested in Foursquare, too.

Systrom's focus was totally on Burbn, testing it out among his friends and working with his investors. Early on, Anderson suggested that Systrom take on a partner in Burbn. It was now spring 2010, and in an effort to remain social while working on his app, Systrom had taken to working on the app at a certain coffee bar. There, he would see Mike Krieger, another Mayfield Fellow. One day, he let Krieger try out Burbn. Perhaps the name struck a chord with Krieger. His father had worked for a number of whiskey companies when he was growing up. Steve Bertoni of *Forbes* reported that Krieger wasn't a fan of location check-in apps, but that Burbn was the first one that he "loved." The feature that most caught his attention was that users could share photos of their check-ins as well as their location.

A month later, Systrom asked Krieger to quit his job at Meebo and become the cofounder of Burbn. They tested how well they worked together first, and not long after, Krieger was in.

In the months that followed, Systrom worried at times that his gut instincts were off. After he left NextStop, Facebook bought the website in July 2010. Soon after, the travel recommendations site was completely gone. Facebook had simply wanted the company for the talent that worked there. For a second time, Systrom was very close to working for the social media giant. Additionally, the NextStop purchase may have called to mind his internship at Odeo. Jack Dorsey, Systrom's officemate at Odeo, had

Zynga, Inc. (whose offices are shown here), is called a social-gaming company because its games are played in conjunction with social media. It was Zynga's game that inspired Systrom early in his career.

begun developing Twitter not long after Systrom worked with him. According to the *Harvard Business Review*, in May 2010, it had more than fifty million users. Systrom told *Vanity Fair*, "I was like, 'Great. I missed the Twitter boat, I missed the Facebook boat.'" The missed opportunities were starting to pile up.

None of this stopped Systrom. He and Krieger were working well together and were about to take a step in a new direction.

CHAPTER 4

The Pivot

With seed money in hand, Systrom met Krieger on his first day as a partner in Burbn with a proposition. He wanted to scrap the whole Burbn project and start anew, a move called a "pivot" in the tech world. Burbn wasn't distinguishing itself as an app in an increasingly crowded marketplace, especially not from Foursquare, which was the hottest location service at the time. Systrom didn't see this as a problem necessarily. He told Austin Carr of *Fast Company* that Burbn "did too much on purpose. We were trying to figure out what got people amped."

The part of Burbn that had stood out to Krieger initially was the photos, not the check-in feature. So the pair honed in on a new idea. "Instead of doing a check-in that had an optional photo, we thought, 'Why don't we do a photo that has an optional check-in?'" Systrom told *Vanity Fair.* The idea wove together Systrom's love of photography

The Cure for What's Ailing Your Photo App

From the start, Instagram set itself apart from other photography or photo filter apps. Krieger has been clear in his belief that when a product solves a problem or anticipates the desires of its potential users, it will succeed. Other photo apps had been criticized for being too slow, not connected to social media sites, and being too reliant on their website. The founders of Instagram aimed to address all of these concerns with their app.

According to the FAQs on Instagram's website, the app solves three problems. First, though cell phone cameras have improved with each new model, mobile photos don't always look great. Instagram filters let photos take on a more "professional" quality. Second, most people are on more than one social media site, and taking the time to share a picture on all of them "is a pain," as the Instagram website reads. Instagram allows users to share images across all their social media platforms at once. Lastly, photo uploading can be cumbersome and take a long time. So Instagram streamlined and hastened the process. "People have better things to do than fumble around with your app," Krieger said in a *Fast Company* article.

(continued on the next page)

(continued from the previous page)

Systrom said in *Forbes* that photo apps before Instagram "asked something" of the users that Instagram took care of *for* them. He likened Instagram's functionality for users to adding a "funny button" to Twitter or a "clever button" to Tumblr. Tumblr is a microblogging and social-networking site owned by Yahoo! on which users can post short blog posts, animations, or just funny images.

In effect, the founders of Instagram carved out a space in the market for themselves by appealing to many different groups with the app. It offers a peek behind the scenes of your favorite musician's tour or a distant friend's trip to Europe. As Jessica Zollman, the former community manager at Instagram, told Nate Bolt of TechCrunch.com, "Instagram can be a window to places and things you don't normally get to see." For wannabe photographers, Instagram allows users to share their creations to however many people they choose and browse through other users' photos for inspiration. Clive Thompson of *Wired* wrote that he believed the appeal of Instagram is all in the filters, which he wrote "help us see the world in a new way."

For now, Instagram has cornered the photo-sharing market. But just as it emerged in a crowded app marketplace filled with photo-editing apps and new social media interfaces, other apps continue to pop up. Facetune, for example, is an iPhone app that helps edit photos to look like they're magazine-ready, smoothing out skin tone, whitening teeth, and erasing wrinkles. Photoshop Touch is the app version of software company Adobe's admired Photoshop program. Could one of these be the next big thing?

and a philosophy Krieger had that developers designing new products should spend time figuring out what people want or the problems they have. By testing Burbn themselves and with friends, the duo had clearly seen that the photo-sharing aspect of Burbn was truly what resonated with their audience the most.

A TEAM, A DREAM, A PLAN

Throughout the summer of 2010, Krieger and Systrom worked on sketching out their app at a renovated pier in San Francisco called Dogpatch Labs. At first, the sketching was literal. Instead of spending a week writing the code for a feature or look that would go unused or be scrapped, they would spend a few hours hand-drawing a picture of

Systrom *(left)* told the AP that they purposely kept the Instagram staff small at the beginning. He would pursue and hire only staffers "who want to build a world-class company."

what they wanted to do. They'd critique and annotate the pieces, making sure they were exactly right before turning them into code. Then Systrom began working on the back-end code, or the parts that support the interface, using much of the Burbn code. Krieger took on designing for the Apple iOS, or operating system, software. Someone who worked at Dogpatch at the same time Systrom and Krieger were there told the *New York Times* that he'd seen them work on the rounded corners of the app's icon for two hours. He called the two "obsessed" with the details of

The iPhone Effect

When Apple released the first iPhone in 2007, it turned the mobile market on its head. It was an iPod with a wider screen and touch controls, a phone, and an Internet-connected device unlike any that had been seen before. It did everything earlier smartphones could do but faster, better, and with additional capabilities. As Steve Jobs, the CEO of Apple at the time, said when he introduced the iPhone: "The iPhone is a revolutionary and magical product that is literally 5 years ahead of any other mobile phone." It cost $499 for the 4GB model and $599 for the 8GB model. The cost was prohibitive for some, but the price for the 8GB dropped to $399 a few months after its June 2007 debut. By June 2008, Apple had sold six million of the iPhone, eventually known as the iPhone 2G, on just four cellphone carriers in four countries. The iPhone had made a splash on the cellphone market—and Apple continued to improve it.

In the story of Instagram, the iPhone 3G is the pivotal model. With the 3G, Apple dropped the price of the iPhone to a more affordable $199 or $299, depending on the size. This gave even more mobile users access to the innovative device. Apple made

(continued on the next page)

(continued from the previous page)

it faster, too. Then the Apple App Store launched in June 2008 and began allowing third-party companies to create apps to be sold there. At the start, the App Store had five hundred apps. Already the technology world knew the App Store was going to be a big deal. Jason Snell of Macworld.com wrote in his review of the 3G that users would be "getting in on the ground floor of the exciting new world of third-party software written for the iPhone." Today, the Apple App Store has more than one million apps, from Instagram and Foursquare, to those created by grocery stores, banks, and the National Weather Service.

During the summer of 2010, when Systrom and Krieger were writing the code for Instagram, they knew a new iPhone was about to hit the market—the iPhone 4. It would have the best mobile camera yet, a great hook for the release of a camera-based app. It also had a faster processor that would make downloading and filtering photos, in addition to Internet posting, more streamlined. By the time Instagram was available, the success of Apple's App Store was clear. Downloading apps was one of the major benefits of buying an iPhone. But other companies—both smartphone makers and software—

weren't going to let Apple corner the market and keep it.

Other app markets began rolling out, such as one for Microsoft's Windows Phone and Google Play, which could be used to download apps on popular devices running the Android operating system. As the competition for smartphone users heated up, Instagram and other app developers suddenly had even more opportunities to reach mobile users. They wanted the loyal iPhone user *and* Android users because though they may not use the same operating systems, they could all still connect on social media. App companies have only been too happy to facilitate linking users of all mobile devices, Instagram included.

their design. Their conscientious time and effort, however, would soon pay off.

FIGURING OUT FILTERS

A challenging two-week push at the Dogpatch office produced a photo-sharing app with the temporary name Codename. Systrom told *Vanity Fair* that after all the hard work, he needed a vacation. He and his girlfriend, Nicole, headed down to Baja California Sur, Mexico. While enjoying the beach with Systrom, Nicole told him she wouldn't use the app he was developing because she didn't take good photos. She mentioned that a friend took much better ones. Systrom assured her the friend wasn't that great of a photographer—he was putting his photos through a filter app, such as Hipstamatic, which was popular at the time. A filter is a photography feature that somehow alters the exposure, lighting, or other qualities of a photo. Systrom told *Vanity Fair* that Nicole then said his app should have a filter feature. The impact of the idea was immediate. Systrom went back to their hotel and hopped online to learn how to write code for a filter. The first filter he created that day gave the colors in the photo more saturation, making them look warmer. He called it X-Pro II. Later, he posted the app's first filtered photo, a dog next to Nicole's foot.

PUTTING IT TOGETHER

It was the final piece to the puzzle. When Systrom got back to the states, he was invigorated by the app's new feature. His knowledge of photography would inform many of the first filters. His experience using the Holga camera while studying abroad in Florence was a particular part of the app's development. "It taught me the beauty of vintage photography and also the beauty of imperfection," Systrom said in *Forbes*. Instagram photos were square, based on the shape of the Holga's photos and those of the more familiar Polaroid. Between the throwback to Polaroid and the filters, Instagram images were both of the present moment

Though much better technology has come along, Polaroid cameras remain of interest to many. Instagram was able to capitalize on that.

and steeped with nostalgia. Krieger told Ellis Hamburger of TheVerge.com that some filters were inspired by aging photos from his and Systrom's childhood and clicking through different Flickr collections. They tried creating about thirty filters, and eleven made it to the app by October 2010, Systrom wrote on Quora.com.

Systrom created many of the first filters. He would first work to create the desired effect on a photo in the photo-editing program Photoshop and then turn it into the proper code. Krieger was working on making the app's user experience the best it could possibly be. Swisher wrote in *Vanity Fair* that Systrom calls Krieger the "soul" of Instagram, especially when it comes to programming. When he and Systrom presented at the University of California, Berkley, Krieger spoke of the importance of entrepreneurs having passion and motivation for their work, the *Daily Cal* reported. TechCrunch.com wrote that at another conference Krieger spoke at, he said "to chase what you're passionate about" when considering a new product or project. He also said insight is "something you're really excited to tell strangers about on the train." Krieger poured his excitement and obvious passion into creating Instagram. It showed. The user-friendly experience would become one of the biggest-selling points of the app.

Krieger and Systrom had decided the app's name after much trial and error. They wanted something that would stand out from the other photo apps out there. It needed to be something that could be easily said and spelled, and thus recommended to a friend. Instagram was a combination of "instant" and "telegram," as it was much like an instant telegram. Also, as Systrom wrote on Quora.com, it "sounded camera-y."

Krieger and Systrom were ready to push the app into the last stage of development. They presented their final idea, Instagram the photo-sharing app with filters, to their investors. Steve Anderson told *Vanity Fair* that he remembers thinking, *"Finally."* He thought they had found the right idea.

CHAPTER 5

Shooting for Success

The first filters in place and the investors happy with the direction, Systrom and Krieger prepared to launch Instagram in the Apple App Store. In total, the final version of the app took about eight weeks to build. They'd been giving it to their friends to test, fixing any problems that came up. About one hundred people used the beta version of Instagram. "Beta" is a term given to a program in development that has the major features the finished product will have but isn't completed yet. Some of the users of Instagram's beta version were those who had also used Burbn.

This was a crucial time for Systrom and Krieger. In choosing whom to give access to Instagram beta, they wanted to find ways to improve the app but also start a little buzz. Systrom and Krieger showed the app to a few media outlets and tech bloggers, as well as other tech developers. Fortunately, the two were well connected in the tech world from their Stanford days and the Mayfield

Fellows Program. MG Siegler from TechCrunch.com wrote a whole preview of the app before it was launched. He declared it "very good," and praised the quality of the photo filters and the social aspect. After using Instagram, Siegler had found some of his favorite filter apps, Hipstamatic and CameraBag, lacking. Reviews like Siegler's surely piqued the interest of the tech-savvy and amateur iPhone photographers alike.

Perhaps the most important user of Instagram's beta version was Jack Dorsey, Systrom's former coworker at Odeo, and the founder of Twitter. He quickly became a

Krieger and Systrom used their connections well and seemed poised for success as Instagram underwent beta testing.

Going Mobile—Only!

Instagram was developed only as an app, an aspect that made it stand out from the beginning. In 2010, even though the Apple App Store and other app markets had been around for a few years, many big companies still weren't looking at apps as a separate kind of software development. Some still hadn't altered their desktop websites for viewing on a mobile device, a phenomenon Steven Bertoni of *Forbes* compared to jamming an "overstuffed suitcase into an overhead bin." And their apps were similarly not taking the smaller screen and processor of mobile devices into consideration. But Instagram did—and at first it didn't have an official website at all.

Part of this choice had to do with the Instagram founders' philosophy about their product. Systrom and Krieger wanted to be incredibly focused on the mobile platform, working to make Instagram the easiest and fastest it could be, without getting bogged down by programming for both the web and the app. Systrom and Krieger also understood the growing mobile market and saw a way to take advantage of the space in it. Systrom wrote on Quora.com that they thought people would be linking to Instagram through other services, perhaps Facebook, and at first they worried about needing the website to bring in users.

The care Krieger and Systrom took in developing Instagram as a mobile-only app was noticed. *Forbes* reported that Matt Cohler, an investor at Benchmark Capital, said Instagram was the first program he'd experienced that felt like it was "truly native to mobile." Cohler went on to call the mobile scaling of the social aspects, interface, and infrastructure to be "nothing short of extraordinary under any circumstance" especially considering the small team working on Instagram.

Eventually, third-party developers began to create websites with Instagram's photostream. Seeing this, it was then that Systrom and Krieger developed Instragram.com. To some in the tech industry, creating a website years after a company puts out a product might seem backward. But, as is the Instagram way, the founders waited until the website answered a need. Systrom knew it was inevitable. He told TechCrunch.com in September 2010 that the web would eventually be part of Instagram. His and Krieger's restraint on the website version demonstrated great skills of prioritization, as well as a good deal of foresight. "Our goal is to not just be a photo-sharing app, but to be the way you share your life when you're on the go," Systrom said, quoted by Christine Lagorio-Chafkin in *Inc*.

champion for the app, using it to post photos to Twitter before the app's official launch.

One part of preparing to launch Instagram in the Apple App Store was creating the app's icon, or the small picture that would represent Instagram on the screen of a mobile device. At first, Systrom designed an icon that looked like an old camera, but that changed before the app launched. Systrom wrote on Quora.com that the changing "came down to branding." The company needed an image that was exclusively their own and would always represent Instagram. One of the first Instagram users, Cole Rise, was the one who came up with the familiar Instagram icon used at the launch and today: a cartoonish, retro single-lens camera with its viewfinder in the upper right-hand corner and a small rainbow in the upper left-hand corner. "Insta" appears below the rainbow.

METEORIC LAUNCH

At midnight on October 6, 2010, the Instagram app went live in the Apple App Store. Going "live" is tech-speak for a web software or app launch. The buzz about the app had built to a roar so loud, Systrom and Krieger had to work twenty-four hours straight at their office at Dogpatch Labs to keep Instagram running. Bits Blog on the *New York Times* website and TechCrunch.com had written about Instagram by 6 AM. Within that day, Instagram had twenty-five thousand users. It outgrew its servers almost immediately, causing Krieger and Systrom to scramble to

It's common for those at tech startups to work long hours right after a product launches. There are always going to be unanticipated problems that need to be solved quickly at this time.

find a way to keep the app humming. Krieger told Kara Swisher of *Vanity Fair* that he guessed about 30 percent of the team's energy was spent keeping the servers running for the first few days after Instagram's meteoric launch and that they relied on Adam D'Angelo for help with some of their early server problems. D'Angelo was the founder of the question-and-answer website Quora.com. Systrom had met D'Angelo at the same Stanford party where he met Mark Zuckerberg, and this connection proved vital after the Instagram launch. Instagram ended up being moved

Startup Investing: What's the Appeal?

Courting investors is a big part of starting a new company. Some investors provide "seed money," a term that calls to mind planting seeds that could grow. This is the funding provided when a startup is just beginning. It aids the company in paying to hire more people, rent an office space, and buy supplies such as the computers and pens used to do work. Investors might give money to a specific project a company is working on, hoping to see it succeed or at least find out something new from it. Investment campaigns may continue at a startup until it begins to turn a profit on its own. Then more funding may be raised when a company wants to expand.

It's clear that investors are a key part of the functioning of a startup. But what's in it for them? It may seem like they're just lending money to untested companies. There are many reasons for a person, company, or investment group to fund a startup. However, the two most common reasons are to make a profit and innovate.

By giving money to a startup, an investor often gets something in return. Some investors become members of a startup's board of directors. They're allowed to have some say in decisions, helping to see their money put to good use. Investors are commonly considered part owners of a company, too. They may be entitled to shares, or parts, of the company should it "go public," or begin to be traded on the stock market.

Often it's individuals or other technology companies that give money to tech startups for reasons of innovation. Jack Dorsey of Twitter, for example, perhaps took the opportunity to invest in Instagram because the two apps were often used together and shared a future on the mobile market. He might want to see what new coding, interface, and user experiences the Instagram team would come up with. In time, Systrom and Krieger's Instagram engineers could find new ways of improving apps. Their successes could help other apps, like Twitter, be better and faster in the future. The other part of innovation ties into investors' business sense, too. Investors will be the first to know when a startup is growing in popularity and would have a relationship with the startups' founders. This could make it easier for the investor to buy the startup and acquire its present technology and talent, or the engineers, designers, and other staff working on it.

(continued on the next page)

(continued from the previous page)

There are always risks when investing, especially in the fast-moving world of technology. The old adage "The greater the risk, the greater the reward" can be true. But for every Facebook or Instagram a company invests in, there are dozens of apps, websites, and software ideas that don't gain enough traction to last. There's also the possibility of overlap. Andreessen Horowitz, a venture capital firm, gave money to Krieger and Systrom when they were still working on Burbn, which, while it contained a photo feature, was closer to Foursquare than a photo app. Andreessen Horowitz, smart investment company that it is, was also funding an up-and-coming photo service called PicPlz. When Systrom and Krieger pivoted to the Instagram idea, Andreessen Horowitz declined to invest in the company further. Andreessen Horowitz viewed the two apps as competitors, and they had been investing in PicPlz as a photo app first. Nonetheless, their initial investment in Burbn would pay as Instagram took off.

entirely onto Amazon EC2, the Amazon Elastic Compute Cloud, to accommodate the quick growth. Amazon EC2 allows for as many virtual servers as a company might need and provides security and storage, too. It was a smart move to choose a server that was able to grow with Instagram. Within the first week, the app had one hundred thousand users. Within a month, that number grew ten times over to one million users.

Systrom told *Inc.*'s Christine Lagorio-Chafkin that he was in awe of the quick growth during the earliest days of Instagram. "We crossed 10,000 users within hours, and I was like, 'This is the best day of my life,'" Systrom said. "At the end of the day, it kept growing so much I thought, 'Are we counting wrong?'" Of course, the numbers weren't wrong. Instagram was an instant hit.

Technology writers continued to buzz about the app, questioning why it was popular and marveling at the quick adoption of app users. Clive Thompson wrote in *Wired* about what he called the "allure" of Instagram, saying, "Instagram made photo sharing drop-dead easy. Plus, photos are the global lingua franca, so the app spread worldwide quickly." *Lingua franca* is a common language spoken when people who speak different languages must communicate with each other. Statements like Thompson's only catapulted Instagram further into the app-world stratosphere. However, before they could go any higher, they needed more money.

GROWTH OF A COMMUNITY

In early 2011, Benchmark Capital, Baseline Ventures, and Lowercase Capital, among others, invested another

$7 million combined in Instagram, which continued to add users. Systrom's friend Jack Dorsey invested, too. D'Angelo also threw his hat in with Instagram. Matt Cohler of Benchmark Capital was vocal about his support for Instagram, telling *Vanity Fair,* "It was very clear [Instagram] was striking a chord and fulfilling an unmet need." After this round of investments, Instagram was being valued at more than $25 million, with about 1.75 million users. Growth within the company wasn't just needed; it was inevitable.

At first, Instagram was just Systrom and Krieger. But as Systrom remarked when he spoke at the 2013 Middlesex School graduation, "Life is a team sport." The company grew to six employees in the months after the Instagram launch, including a much-needed "community evangelist" named Jessica Zollman, hired in July 2011. The number of Instagram users had gotten too large for Systrom and Krieger to manage. Zollman's job, often called the community manager at similar companies, was primarily to work with Instagram users on- and offline. The team doubled its size over the next year. Krieger wrote on the White House Blog about his contentment with the company's growth: "There are few better sights than walking into an office full of talented, hard-working folks, working together to build a great company from the ground up."

Matt Cohler of Benchmark Capital was an early supporter of Instagram. Through his efforts, Benchmark became one of Instagram's biggest investors.

Instagram moved into a small office space in the South Park area of San Francisco, near the Giants' baseball field, AT&T Park. They called it "the cave," according to the *Los Angeles Times*. It was their nearness to the park that helped Systrom and Krieger realize how big Instagram had gotten. Systrom told Kara Swisher of *Vanity Fair* that during a playoff game soon after Instagram's launch, they could hear the home runs being hit. So they searched on Instagram to see if anyone was at the game and posting pictures of it to get a sense of what it would be like to be there. Systrom said they found that about 140 photos had been taken and shared in the previous two hours at the park. "That was the moment we realized Instagram could be far more than photo sharing," he told Swisher.

CHAPTER 6

The Big Offer

Throughout 2011, Instagram added about one million users a month, according to Austin Carr of *Fast Company*. On Quora.com, Systrom said the app was even attracting many users from Europe and Asia, highlighting the "language-agnostic characteristics of photos," meaning there's no need to speak the same language to enjoy photos from other countries' users.

Instagram's growth thrilled Systrom and Krieger, but it didn't come without sacrifice. Systrom told *Forbes* that the app "keeps us up at night and wakes us up in the morning." Since the Instagram team remained small, everyone was on call in case any problems occurred. Each engineer was required to have his MacBook with wireless card close by at all times for troubleshooting—even during dates, weddings, and birthday parties. Krieger told interview website *The Setup* that he even took his MacBook Air with him on hikes and long bike rides.

SPREADING THE WORD

As Instagram grew, developers started to build software that used Instagram. Followgram.com, for example, created a website for the app, since Instagram was still mobile-only at the time. Software developers can create products powered by an app or website using its application-programming interface (API). An API includes the instructions and standards that give someone access to the software of an app or website. For Instagram, the API would give developers access to the photostream and comments users make on photos. Systrom wrote on Quora.com in January 2011 that they wanted to encourage developers to do so—but not until the official API was released. At that time, Systrom said the private API still changed too much. He and Krieger were still constantly improving their code. Running an app or site on an outdated API could "break" developers' Instagram products. That would create a bad experience for both the developers and all their users. Systrom wrote, "Our first responsibility is to the quality of service of our site and the protection of data for our users."

Shortly after he wrote this on Quora.com, the public API was released, introducing a whole new crop of Instagram-based apps including Instant Album, Carousel, and Extragram. Developers like Systrom and Krieger want third parties to use their API. It gives them ideas for future features and often brings in more users, too.

Instagram also introduced hashtags in February 2011, a phenomenon that had begun on Twitter and was much later rolled out on Facebook. The app had 1.75 million users who were now able to use a hashtag, or pound sign (#), before a word or phrase to tag a brand, emotion, or phrase. Or the hashtag could act as a way to just identify things in the photo. On February 2, 2011, Krieger posted a picture on Instagram of his cat, tagging it #cat. In the blog post introducing the hashtags, Instagram explained how the hashtag could be used in many ways. Clicking on a hashtag—such as #cat—would allow a user

Instagram's appeal includes being able to tag popular brands, emotions, or phrases in photo captions. What hashtag could these girls use with their picture?

Instagram's Rich and Famous

The hashtag corresponded with an influx of another kind of brand—celebrities. From skateboarder Tony Hawk to U.S. president Barack Obama, the rich and famous on Instagram have some of the highest numbers of followers. It's easy to guess why Instagram users follow celebrities. Americans have always been interested in the minutiae of celebrities' lifestyles. Diet tips, clothing, and vacation photos have long appeared on the pages of the magazines lining grocery store checkouts. Instagram removes the middleman of tabloids and gives people a peek into celebrities' lives without paying anything—at least, for the pictures.

Instagram is a modern vehicle of promotion for celebrities using the app. First, it's a free way to let the public know about an upcoming book, movie, or appearance on a TV show. Second, Instagram-using celebs can keep a constant stream of content flowing to their fans. In the fast-moving world of Internet popular culture, it's easy to get lost among the great host of news available to users about celebrities, not to mention their friends' posts on social media sites. With Instagram, a celebrity need only take a moment to remain part of the glut of pop culture consumption. Of course, with the frequency that some post, they must just find it fun to play with the filters, just like other people do.

What celebrities say or show on Instagram is another reason they'd find the app appealing. Assuming a famous person has control over his or her own Instagram account (some may pay a public relations person to post on their behalf), the celeb him- or herself chooses what is written or photographed. Celebs controlling the message is something unheard of in the world of frenzied paparazzi, *E! News*, and PerezHilton.com. In addition, their posts can help reflect to fans and followers their humanity. Those in the spotlight may be seen as arrogant or their wealth and notoriety viewed with disdain. Through Instagram, celebrities can show that they're relatable and, like magazines often exclaim, "Just like us!"

Whatever their reason for using Instagram, Justin Bieber, Rihanna, and so many others have gathered millions of followers. They're prolific and, apparently, just as enthralled with the app as everyone else.

to see all the photos with the same hashtag. Organizations, publications, and brands soon latched on to the hashtags as a way to promote and watch their product or idea being circulated among users. Instagram's introductory blog post included National Public Radio's call for photos using #love and #hate with photos capturing each. It also listed Brisk Iced Tea's #briskpic campaign during the 2011 SXSW (South by Southwest) Festival, which asked users to tag photos of themselves holding Brisk cans. The photos would be posted on a website and maybe featured on a future can of Brisk. Soon, Instagram posts were full of hashtags, including brands, funny phrases, and inside jokes between users. Sometimes the hashtags took the place of photo captions or comments altogether.

APRIL 2012

In the first part of 2012, Instagram had thirty million iPhone users. Then, in April 2012, an Instagram app for Android launched. One million users downloaded it in just one day, *Vanity Fair* reported. According to BBC News, that grew to five million total over six days.

At this point, Krieger was in charge of the technology behind the scenes, while Systrom, as CEO, took on a more visible role. He worked on improving Instagram, but also talking to investors—including those who wanted to buy Instagram.

Roelof Botha, an investor with Sequoia Capital, contacted Systrom in early 2012. Already invested in Tumblr and other social media sites, Botha had noticed how well Instagram was retaining users. It impressed him. Botha wanted to quickly put $50 million into Instagram, Kara Swisher reported in *Vanity Fair*. Botha wasn't alone in his awareness of how well Instagram was doing. He was just one suitor Systrom dealt with at the beginning of 2012—Facebook's CEO Mark Zuckerberg was another.

TWITTER TALK

However, the first big offer Instagram received came from Jack Dorsey of Twitter. Dorsey, already an investor in Instagram and a frequent user, had consistently shown interest in the app's growth. He'd tried to initiate talks of purchase beginning the previous year after observing Instagram slowly nearing Twitter's number of users. It was clear that mobile app users regularly used the Twitter and Instagram apps together. With these observations in mind, in addition to his friendship with Systrom, Dorsey may have seen the acquisition of Instagram as inevitable. But Systrom hadn't been open to discussing changes in Instagram ownership in 2011. Nonetheless, at the beginning of April 2012, Dorsey and Systrom met up at a conference in Arizona. One evening during the conference, Dorsey and Twitter's chief financial officer (now former) Ali Rowghani, sat around a bonfire together. They pitched an idea to Systrom. They wanted to buy Instagram for around $500 million in restricted stock and common stock.

Swisher wrote in *Vanity Fair* that there's some confusion about that night. Dorsey said Systrom was given an official offer, including a paper listing the terms of the deal. Systrom said that's not the case. He says it was simply a verbal offer. Either way, a few days later—April 4, 2012—Systrom turned the offer down. He planned to take the $50 million investment from Botha at Sequoia Capital. Instagram would remain its own company.

FACEBOOK CALLS

Then Mark Zuckerberg called Systrom. The two had been in touch in the years between Systrom turning down the job offer at Facebook and 2012, so hearing from Zuckerberg didn't come as much of a surprise to Systrom. Systrom had told him Instagram was going to remain an independent company, considering his acceptance of the Sequoia Capital money. Zuckerberg continued to pursue his interest in Instagram, and Systrom ended up at Zuckerberg's house two days later to talk. Zuckerberg made his offer—$1 billion, part of which would be $300 million cash. The offer doubled what Instagram had been purportedly worth, and what Twitter had offered.

The history of Facebook, especially its photo features, sheds light on Zuckerberg's desire to buy Instagram. In the fall of 2005, Facebook, which had launched the previous year and was totally transforming social media, added a photo feature. The ability to add photos was immediately

Mark Zuckerberg has become much more than the founder of Facebook. He's the face of the company often speaking in the press about technology and the future of social media.

popular with users. Over time, they were able to comment on photos and click a button to "like" a photo or status update, essentially giving it a thumbs up. Users could tag their friends, too, or identify a person's face in a photo. In September 2006, Facebook launched its News Feed feature that showed users' friends photos and status updates all in one place. By 2014, Facebook reported that about four hundred billion photos had been shared on Facebook.

Music artists Ne-Yo (left) and Cher Lloyd (right) asked their social media followers to share some ways to keep positive using a hashtag on Facebook, Twitter, and Instagram. Then they used the responses to write a song!

The continual upload of photos by friends is one of the major reasons users spend so long browsing Facebook—and the company needs it to stay that way. The longer users are on the site, the more ads they're exposed to, helping make the site profitable. But Facebook also has games, groups, and more to keep users engaged on the site. Adam D'Angelo of Quora.com, who formerly worked as Facebook's chief technology officer, told Steven Bertoni of *Forbes* that Facebook is a "bundle" of different things. "But it turns out that people just like photos more than anything else," D'Angelo said. "So if you specialize in photos and do photos really well, that's in some way more powerful than this bundle of everything else." Systrom and Krieger had passionately embraced this idea early on. To a brilliant tech mind like Zuckerberg, their choice would have been noticeable.

Instagram took the most-loved feature of Facebook and made it look better and easier to use. Systrom said in *Fast Company* that posting an Instagram photo was a tweet and status update rolled into one. This was part of the reason Instagram was seen as a potential rival to Facebook's social networking dominance. Through the dozen-plus filters available on Instagram, everyday photos could become photographic art. The speed and ease of upload was significant, a change from the clumsy photo feature on Facebook. And even though

Instagram was driving traffic to Facebook through the sharing features of the app, it was noticeably the right traffic. Instagram had the attention of users under age twenty-five, a coveted group Facebook was losing. *Fast Company* reported that Facebook acknowledged in its annual report to the U.S. Securities and Exchange Commission (SEC) that younger users were interacting less with Facebook and more with other sites. In effect, Facebook was becoming less "cool." Instagram was the new, hip kid on the scene, and it was easy for Zuckerberg to imagine it taking over. Instead, he planned to take *it* over instead.

CHAPTER 7

Bought!

The Facebook offer fresh in his mind, Systrom immediately called Krieger when he left Zuckerberg's house. Krieger hopped on a train from San Francisco to Palo Alto, where he met Systrom on the platform. The offer Zuckerberg had presented was part cash, and the rest would be pre-IPO stock, meaning that when Facebook went public, the Instagram founders would be part owners, like other shareholders.

Instagram would be the largest acquisition Facebook had ever made. It was unique in another way as well. It would be the first time Zuckerberg hadn't taken the helm of a company he acquired. During their conversation about the Facebook offer, Zuckerberg had told Systrom that Instagram could function independently within Facebook. For both Zuckerberg and the Instagram founders, this promise was a risk. Zuckerberg had to believe in Systrom and Krieger enough to let them run their part of the business well. Systrom and Krieger had to have faith in Zuckerberg's word. This

The Facebook IPO

Mark Zuckerberg's first moves toward acquiring Instagram came soon after Facebook announced plans to go public in May 2012. "Going public" means a company will be traded on the stock market. The first time a company offers shares for sale is called an IPO, or initial public offering. The U.S. Securities and Exchange Commission (SEC) forces companies to go public once they have five hundred shareholders. At this time, they're obligated to disclose the company's financial information to those shareholders. According to *Business Insider* writer Nicholas Carlson, the primary reason the SEC wants companies to share their financial information is to protect the shareholders. Before going public, a company doesn't need to share any financial information, so the risk of owning shares is greater and is mostly undertaken by a group the SEC calls accredited investors. Accredited investors are quite wealthy, including, by the SEC definition, people with a net worth of more than $1 million. Once a company has five hundred investors, the SEC assumes that some of a company's shares will have trickled down to people of more modest means. The SEC wants them to have the best information they can to make decisions about their investments. Going public also opens a company to more of these lower-level investors, offering opportunities for them to make money.

Once the Facebook IPO was announced, focus on the problem areas of the social media site sharpened. Instagram was seen as a possible remedy to Facebook's biggest weakness: mobile devices. Carr reported in *Fast Company* that Facebook had spent millions of dollars on creating Facebook apps using web technology, something Instagram had eschewed early on. The company tried to create an app that would work across all mobile devices, instead of focusing on excellence for a few. Zuckerberg, Carr wrote, said it was the "biggest strategic mistake" Facebook ever made. It was clearly problematic, as the *Wall Street Journal* reported that about half of Facebook users access Facebook on their mobile device. The lack of immediate monetization—or Facebook's ability to make money on its mobile products—was one reason the social media giant gave for not focusing on mobile sooner.

Instagram, on the other hand, had an impressive mobile interface designed for the best user experience from the beginning, a specialty of Krieger's. Not only was it successful in its mobile technology, but it also was showing that a company doing *only*

(continued on the next page)

(continued from the previous page)

mobile could be successful. By acquiring Instagram, Facebook could have a new opportunity to capture the mobile market, both with Facebook and by owning the popular Instagram. The purchase would be a way to bolster the company before shares could be bought or sold, and perhaps act as a promise to buyers that Facebook was still viable, growing, and most important, relevant.

The Facebook-Instagram deal could be compared to Google's acquisition of YouTube in 2006. While the $1.6 billion Google spent on the video website seemed a lot at the time, Google has been able to better its video presence online and introduce new kinds of advertising to create revenue. Instagram had the potential to be that kind of game-changing acquisition for Facebook.

may have been hard for Systrom. He and another Instagram employee named Josh Riedel had both worked at NextStop, which Facebook acquired in 2010—and immediately shut down.

Systrom and Krieger talked on the drive back to San Francisco and made the decision together: they would take Zuckerberg's offer.

JOINING A GIANT

Believing their move was the right one and that Zuckerberg would keep his word about Instagram's independence, Krieger and Systrom closed the deal with Facebook in September 2012. They then moved their offices from San Francisco to the Facebook campus in Menlo Park, California. According to the *New York Times*, a vice president at Facebook preserved the moment with a photo he took using Instagram.

All told, the deal ended up equaling closer to $700 million than $1 billion. It still included the $300 million

Zuckerberg has an Instagram profile—@zuck! As of June 2014, he had more than 83,500 followers.

cash, but the rest, which had been offered in pre-IPO shares, was worth less as Facebook's shares decreased in value on the stock market in the months between the offer and the deal's closing date. A few million lost didn't seem to faze Krieger and Systrom as Zucker-berg appeared from the outset to be making good on his promise to allow the founders to grow Instagram independently.

BAD WITH THE GOOD

The acquisition did have some stumbling blocks as it progressed, however. To begin with, Systrom turned down Jack Dorsey and Twitter mere days before accept-ing Facebook's offer to buy Instagram. Dorsey, who told *Vanity Fair* that he thought Instagram was "a joy to use" and was "blown away by how much detail they put into the experience," was shocked when Instagram announced the sale on April 9, 2012—five days after telling Twitter no. Systrom didn't call Dorsey to tell him about it, and at the time that Dorsey spoke to *Vanity Fair* in 2013, the two hadn't talked much since. Nor has Dorsey used Instagram to post to his Twitter account since, something he did frequently before the Facebook deal. Twitter tried briefly to fight for the right to Ins-tagram in court, mostly based on the conversation and possible paper offer between Systrom and Dorsey in

Arizona. Nothing came of the suit, though. Twitter *did* remove a feature that allowed users to "follow" people on Instagram via Twitter. Instagram then removed some of its Twitter technology support, keeping the best versions of photos only on Instagram. It wasn't the sweetest of partings.

Shortly after closing the Facebook deal, a change in Instagram's terms of service caused users to threaten to delete the app. Users believed the Instagram team was giving themselves permission to sell user photos. According to the *Wall Street Journal*, the sentence that users were questioning read: "To help us deliver interesting paid or sponsored content or promotions, you agree that a business may pay Instagram to display your username, likeness, photos (along with any associated metadata) and/or actions you take, in connection with paid or sponsored content or promotions without any compensation to you." The statement was easily misinterpreted. It seemed to mean that Instagram could allow companies to use photos or information from users' accounts in advertisements, though companies wouldn't have full license to do what they wanted with them. As Nilay Patel described on TheVerge.com, "Budweiser can put up a box in the timeline that says 'Our favorite Instagram photos of this bar!' and put user photos there, but it can't take those photos and modify

Systrom told *Business of Fashion* in 2014 that he thought joining Facebook made both stronger: "When a social company and a social company come together with different ways of approaching the same mission, that is when you end up getting the value of bringing two things together."

them, or combine them to create a new thing." Users reacted immediately to the change, heading to Twitter and declaring their feelings of betrayal loud and clear.

Many users didn't understand that the new terms of service had actually increased limitations surrounding Instagram photos and advertising. But the terms of service had been written by the Facebook legal team and were released without fanfare or explanation. Patel and other technology bloggers wrote that the acquisition by Facebook had made people wary, since it seemed for a time that Facebook was

The Privacy Problem

A larger social media issue emerges with Instagram's terms of service problem: privacy.

Privacy on social media has long troubled parents and teachers who worry about teens' online presence. Advertisers having access to photos and other information is a fairly new concern, growing with the increased effort to monetize social media sites, such as Facebook and Twitter. The Pew Research Center reported in 2013 that parents are generally more concerned than teens about advertisers accessing a user's Internet activities. But adults also worry that teens give out too much information based on location, age, and friends that could easily be used to harm them.

On the other hand, teen social media users have grown up using these sites and have an awareness of the information they're broadcasting. According to the Pew Research Center findings, 60 percent of teenage Facebook users have private profiles and say they have "high levels of confidence in their ability to manage settings." These settings, which are similar on other social networking sites, include blocking those a user isn't connected with on the site from seeing parts or all of his or her profile, sharing pictures only with a select group, and prohibiting

(continued on the next page)

(continued from the previous page)

anyone using a search engine to find a profile just by searching for a user's name. Monitoring these settings as social media sites change over time is smart. As the sites update, so might the privacy settings, and they could change back to the default settings despite what a user has set previously.

Privacy settings notwithstanding, sharing any content on social media sites, even with people you trust, is a risk. User content can easily be shared with others with the click of a button, or saved and shown to others offline. Keeping this in mind when posting a photo on Instagram or writing an angry status on Facebook can be beneficial for users of all ages. You may be able to delete a post the next day, but that doesn't mean someone hasn't saved it or taken a screenshot.

However, the downfalls of Internet privacy may work to a user's advantage if cyberbullying occurs. Cyberbullying is any time technology—such as texting or social media—is used to threaten or harm someone. No matter how hurtful comments or photos may be, always save any instances of cyberbullying directed at you. They can be used as evidence when you involve an adult in the problem, something you should do immediately before the cyberbullying gets worse. Users are responsible for their online actions, and in cases of cyberbullying on social media, courts have upheld harassment claims.

Anyone using a social media site should be aware that his or her photos on Instagram or tweets may be viewed by strangers, advertisers, or even friends and family members who weren't the intended audience. Privacy settings are helpful, but not foolproof, so caution is always the wisest course online.

always trying to find a way to generate revenue using its users' information. Systrom told *Vanity Fair* he should have questioned the need for the sentence at issue, as Instagram wasn't yet using advertising on the app. The angry user response prompted Systrom to write a post on the Instagram blog titled, "Thank you, and we're listening." It not only apologized for the confusion but also explained that Instagram was looking to add "innovative advertising" in the future and wanted to have a structure in place for it. The post clarified that advertisers would not be allowed to use user photos and

Twitter users have the option of making their tweets public or protecting them. Protected tweets go out only to those a user specifies.

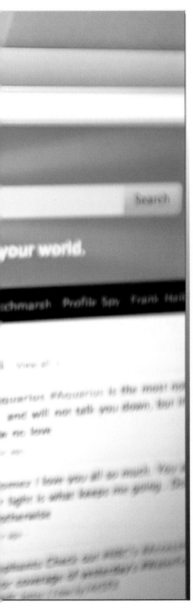

that the terms of service would be edited to omit the part that caused the question to come up.

Systrom spoke about the trust he believes users need to have in Instagram to the *Daily Cal* at the University of California, Berkley: "Trust and privacy are the two things you need to have because you're making effectively a deal with the consumer that they'll use your product." He added, "They will only keep doing that if they trust you." Instagram's quick response to user inquiry helped the controversy pass quickly.

The terms of service and Twitter troubles aside, Instagram's transition into the Facebook family began to show promise quickly. The number of active users increased by more than 1,000 percent, numbering one hundred million by June 2013, just two-and-a-half years since it launched, according to *Vanity Fair*. By comparison, Twitter had only just reached two hundred million at the end of 2012 after six years.

CHAPTER 8

A Future at Facebook

Under the Facebook umbrella, Instagram and its founders have benefitted greatly. Krieger told Austin Carr of *Fast Company* that by working with Facebook engineers, they had "cut out a year in terms of trial and error." The mammoth company has given Instagram access to better public relations, legal counsel, and spam-fighting power, too. Since Systrom and Krieger didn't have to worry about these areas anymore, they had more time to develop a photo-tagging feature and improve Instagram in other ways. They launched a new fifteen-second video feature in June 2013 to compete with Vine, a Twitter company. Instagram gained a search feature called Explore as well. In kind, Facebook's mobile features have benefitted from the app-specific talents of the Instagram team. The scroll feature on the Android's Facebook mobile platform, for example, was adapted directly from the Instagram feed.

Founded in June 2012, Vine was purchased by Twitter in October 2012 for $30 million. It launched the next year in app stores and became the most popular video-sharing app on the market.

All the independent and cooperative progress hasn't gone unnoticed by Zuckerberg. The Instagram team was stationed in the same building as his office. Carr reported in *Fast Company* that Systrom and Zuckerberg are just a short walk from one another and meet about three times a week to discuss new happenings in the tech world and with Instagram.

The extreme growth in Instagram users since joining Facebook necessitated hiring more employees, increasing to thirty-four in mid-2013, and then fifty by the end of that year. The operation was still reflective of the small-team atmosphere of early Instagram. When Facebook reached one hundred million users, it had six hundred employees. Instagram remained a fraction of that. When speaking at the University of California, Berkley, Krieger emphasized how well the company stayed together through the Facebook buy. "We're basically a startup within a larger company," he said, quoted in the *Daily Cal.* The work was continual, though. Krieger likened working on the app to painting a bridge to Ellis Hamburger of TheVerge.com, "You go from one end to the other, and once you're done optimizing and improving your systems, you have to start all over," he said.

THE LIFE OF SUCCESS

Even while Systrom and Krieger's commitment to improving Instagram remained steadfast, not everything stayed the same for the app's founders. *Fast Company* reported

Big names in the tech world often find that celebrity accompanies their product's growth. As CEO of Apple, Steve Jobs was one of the most visible representatives of a company in the tech industry. Instagram's founders would stumble upon similar fame.

that after the acquisition, Systrom's net worth was close to $400 million. As Instagram exploded onto the app scene, Systrom had gotten used to being more visible. Just months after the Instagram launch, he sat in the fourth row as Steve Jobs presented Instagram during an Apple keynote speech. But after the acquisition, Systrom's name became well known beyond the tech world, too. He was invited to red carpet events, such as nightclub openings and fashion shows in places like London, England. *Fast Company* reported that Systrom even got to travel to Tokyo, Japan, and Paris, France! In 2013, Systrom was named to the *Time* 100, a list published by the magazine including who it thinks the one hundred most influential people in the world are. TV host Ryan Seacrest praised Systrom and Instagram in the *Time* 100 issue: "Kevin has already left an indelible mark on our culture before reaching the age of 30. I can't wait to see what he dreams up next." Systrom spent time with celebrities, like actor Adrian Grenier and Seacrest, who were big fans of Instagram. Systrom was becoming a celebrity himself, much like Zuckerberg had when Facebook became a worldwide phenomenon.

Krieger gained about $100 million in the wake of the Facebook deal. Kara Swisher of *Vanity Fair* called Krieger the "invisible man of the Instagram story" due to his smaller presence in the general media. However, Krieger has given a number of talks at tech conferences, both with and without Systrom. He's also been active in encouraging young entrepreneurs in Silicon Valley, particularly immigrants like himself. He attended the 2012 State of the Union address, sitting with First Lady Michelle Obama, and was referenced by the president in a speech on immigration reform. Krieger wrote on the White House Blog that his Brazilian background made becoming a U.S. entrepreneur more difficult, and that he supports new programs that help foreign students in technology, science, and math fields study and train in the United States. "Innovation happens best when people of different backgrounds come together to solve the world's toughest challenges," he wrote.

Systrom has been outspoken about entrepreneurship as well. In an interview with the alumni magazine for the Middlesex School, Systrom emphasized the importance of doing a job you love, something he's found in working with technology, raising the money for it, and working with talented engineers. He spoke of a belief in learning from what doesn't work, too, saying that it's essential to work hard: "Entrepreneurship is really not about divine inspiration."

The pair needs to save some inspiration for themselves. Instagram remains a huge player in social networking today—and it has yet to create any revenue. It took Facebook until 2009 to become profitable, about five years after launching. Instagram is only about four years old, so the time is coming to try and turn a profit. As Instagram

Adding Ads

In the Instagram blog post explaining the new terms of service, Systrom wrote: "We envision a future where both users and brands alike may promote their photos & accounts to increase engagement and to build a more meaningful following." He and Krieger always intended Instagram to be a business that turned a profit. Of course, any advertising on Instagram would have to follow the same philosophy of other Instagram features: it would have to solve a problem or answer a need of users. Emily White was hired as the director of business operations to begin exploring that topic and figure out how to turn the Instagram philosophy into dollars.

Since Instagram's inception, brands have used the photo-sharing app to broadcast their product. Brands, like early adopters Pepsi and Red Bull, simply sign up, share photos, and add followers, just like other Instagram users. When Instagram introduced hashtags in February 2011, brands began to see the marketing potential of Instagram. They could actually see how far their photos were going through a hashtag's repeated use by users. Austin Carr of *Fast Company* speculated that selling hashtags could be one way to bring in money from advertisers. Then if a user tagged a photo, for example, #iloveshoes, the shoe company that owned the hashtag could easily include photos of its beautiful shoes in the user's feed.

Any advertising used on Instagram would have to fit the look of the app, too. Systrom likened his wants for potential advertising to *Vogue*, in which the ads are as glossy and fabulous as the editorial photographs. Brands' Instagram-like images could create a cycle of the need-based advertising Systrom wants. A company purchases the hashtag #iloveshoes. A user posts a picture of shoes he loves, using the hashtag. The company, which would be tracking the hashtag, inserts a gorgeous picture of its shoes in the user's feed. The user clicks on the photo and buys the shoes. Then the cycle repeats. But this is just one idea of many that Instagram could adopt in order to make ads work.

Instagram added its first round of advertising to users over age eighteen on November 1, 2013. The company wrote on the Instagram blog that it wanted the ads to feel natural and started with brands already part of Instagram. Users again went to Twitter to post complaints. But whether or not users want them, Instagram has to turn a profit—and the ads appear to be effective for marketers thus far. In fact, in March

(continued on the next page)

(continued from the previous page)

2014, Facebook made a deal with a big ad agency called Omnicom regarding advertising on Instagram. Omnicom represents brands such as AT&T and Pepsi. According to FoxBusiness.com, the deal was uniquely structured to Instagram: Omnicom will work *with* Instagram to create ads suitable for the app.

White's challenge, no matter the advertising format or content, is to make sure Instagram stays "cool" even though it's making money. The Pew Research Center reported that teens feel they could "better express themselves" on Twitter and Instagram. They're part of a key group of consumers for advertisers, and should advertising be too overt or change the Instagram experience too much, can easily be lost.

remains a free app, advertising is the most likely way to generate revenue.

Mobile advertising has been a tough sell for many companies. Luckily, it's one that Facebook has just begun to successfully explore. According to *Fast Company*, 25 percent of Facebook's sales in the first quarter of 2013 were from mobile revenue. That means Instagram will at least have some experienced help behind its initial efforts. Nonetheless, the Instagram team has a challenge ahead of it.

LOOKING BACK BUT GOING FORWARD

Looking back on the Facebook-Instagram deal almost two years later, many have called the Facebook's acquisition a bargain. Jenna Wortham of the *New York Times* reported that Benchmark Capital thought Instagram could have been a successful company on its own or held out for a higher offer. *Business Insider* reported that one well-known startup investor, Shervin Pishevar, tweeted that Instagram would be worth upwards of $5 billion had it remained an independent company. Pishevar's tweet went on to praise Facebook's leader: "Insanely smart, cheap acquisition by Zuck." Surely Zuckerberg feels the same. The continual sharing of technology and potentially users are two of the practical reasons for Zuckerberg to be pleased about his buy. Steven Bertoni of *Forbes* quoted Quora.com's Adam D'Angelo on a major advantage of the Instagram purchase: "It was probably very scary to Facebook that someone else might own Instagram or that it might turn into its own social network." Today, the two are no longer rivals, but partners working toward the same goals—and fearing the same threats.

At the beginning of 2014, Instagram introduced Instagram Direct, a messaging service that allows users to send pictures and video to particular users, and not share them with their whole network. According to the Instagram blog post: "There are... moments in our lives we want to share, but that will be the most relevant only to a smaller group of people—an inside joke between friends captured on the go, a special family moment or even just one more photo of your new puppy. Instagram Direct helps you share these moments." While the idea might be a natural extension of Instagram, Instagram Direct seems to be a reaction to the quick photo-messaging app Snapchat. Snapchat appeared on the app scene in September 2011, another startup dream from two young tech savants. Snapchat is just one example of the continually growing app market that Instagram's founders, with the big-brother backing of Facebook, must face. After four years of hard work, Krieger and Systrom have shown to be more than willing to try and stay ahead of their competitors.

THE BRIGHT FUTURE

Kevin Systrom sees Instagram—and technology like it—as the movement of the future, bringing the events of the whole world to any user, any time. "Imagine the power of surfacing what's happening in the world through images, and potentially other types of media in the future, to each and every person who holds a mobile phone," Systrom told Steven Bertoni in *Forbes*. He's invested for the long run, even working to improve himself for the benefit

Krieger and Systrom won a Webby Award in May 2012. The Webby Awards honor outstanding contributions to tech and Internet culture each year.

of the company: *Gawker* and other news outlets have reported that he's working toward his master's in business administration (MBA). He and Krieger have seen the user base grow to about one hundred fifty million in 2014 and released the app for Microsoft's Windows Phone as well.

Instagram's founders have engaged those one hundred fifty million Instagram users with sharing their lives in a new way. From Justin Bieber photographing traffic in Los Angeles to high school students posting selfies of their new haircuts, Instagram has crossed the boundaries of age, interest, and even social class. There have never been more ways for people to interact online, and yet so many choose Instagram as their network of choice. It could be the filters that make users look at the world with new beauty. Maybe it does come down to the ease of use in the mobile interface. Undoubtedly, it's partly Systrom's and Krieger's individual passions and signatures on Instagram that has kept users coming back for more. As Systrom said in an interview with the Middlesex School's alumni journal, "It's very difficult to make something that people love. The smartest people in the world can put products out that don't capture peoples hearts." Instagram has—in billions of photos taken by millions around the world.

Fact Sheet on

INSTAGRAM

Date launched: October 6, 2010

Founded by: Mike Krieger and Kevin Systrom

CEO: Kevin Systrom

Investors: Baseline Ventures, Andreessen Horowitz, Jack Dorsey, Adam D'Angelo, Sequoia Capital, Benchmark Capital, Lowercase Capital

Owned by: Facebook, Inc.

Official date of Facebook purchase: September 6, 2012

Final cost of purchase: About $700 million

Number of Employees: 50 (as of September 2013)

Headquarters: 1 Hacker Way
Menlo Park, California 94025

Current revenue: $0

Estimated revenue for 2014: $340 million (from Evercore analysts)

Devices and platforms where instagram is available: Instagram.com, Apple App Store for iPhones, Google Play for Android phones, Microsoft Windows Phone Store for the Windows Phone (as of March 2014)

Services Instagram is compatible with: Flickr, Facebook, Twitter; Foursquare if a user includes a location with his or her photo

Number of users: 150 million (as of March 2014)

Percentage of users outside the United States: About 60 percent

Languages supported by Instagram: Afrikaans, Chinese, Czech, Danish, Dutch, English, Finnish, French, German, Greek, Indonesian, Italian, Japanese, Korean, Malay, Norwegian, Polish, Portuguese, Russian, Spanish, Swedish, Tagalog, Thai, and Turkish

Total photos shared: 16 billion

Average number of photos shared per day: 55 million

Most Instagram followers: Justin Bieber 14,799,343 (as of March 2014)

Other top Instagram users: Kim Kardashian, more than 13 million followers; Rihanna, more than 12 million followers; Beyoncé, more than 10.5 million followers; Miley Cyrus, more than 9.5 million followers; Ariana Grande, more than 9 million followers (as of March 2014)

KEVIN SYSTROM

Date of birth: December 30, 1983

Birthplace: Holliston, Massachusetts

Parents: Doug and Diane Systrom

Current residence: San Francisco, California

Net worth: $400 million

Marital status: Single

High school attended: Holliston High School, the Middlesex School

College attended: Stanford University

Major: Management science and engineering

Degree earned: Bachelor of science (BS)

Internship: Podcast company Odeo

First job: Associate product marketing manager and corporate development associate, Google, Inc.

Position at Instagram: CEO

Instagram username: @kevin

Number of followers: More than 1 million (as of March 2014)

Fact Sheet on

MIKE KRIEGER

Date of birth: March 4, 1986

Birthplace: São Paolo, Brazil

Came to the United States: 2004

Current residence: San Francisco, California

Net worth: $100 million

Marital status: Single

College attended: Stanford University

Major: Symbolic systems

Degrees earned: Bachelor of science (BS), master of science (MS)

Internships: Microsoft, Foxmarks, Inc.

First job: User experience designer and engineer, Meebo, Inc.

Position at Instagram: Lead software engineer

Instagram username: @mikeyk

Number of followers: More than 170,000 (as of March 2014)

Timeline

December 30, 1983: Kevin Systrom is born in Holliston, Massachusetts.

March 4, 1986: Mike Krieger is born in São Paolo, Brazil.

1999: Systrom starts at the Middlesex School.

2002: Systrom graduates high school, enrolls at Stanford University.

2004: Krieger enrolls at Stanford University.

December 2004–March 2005: Systrom studies abroad in Florence, Italy.

Spring 2005: Systrom enters the Mayfield Fellows Program.

Summer 2005: Systrom interns at Odeo, meeting Jack Dorsey; Mark Zuckerberg offers him a job at Facebook.

May 2006: Systrom graduates from Stanford with a BS in management science and engineering; he begins work at Google.

June–September 2006: Krieger interns at Microsoft.

Spring 2007: Krieger enters the Mayfield Fellows Program.

June–September 2007: Krieger interns at Foxmarks, Inc.

2008: Krieger graduates from Stanford with a BS and MS in symbolic systems.

January 2009: Krieger begins working for Meebo.

Spring 2009: Systrom leaves his job at Google to work for NextStop.

January 2010: Systrom meets Steven Anderson at a party; Anderson invests in Burbn; Systrom leaves NextStop to work on Burbn full-time.

March 2010: Krieger signs with Systrom as cofounder of Burbn.

May 2010: Krieger leaves Meebo.

Summer 2010: Krieger and Systrom rent an office space at Dogpatch Labs; Systrom creates the first Instagram filter.

October 6, 2010: Instagram launches in the Apple App Store to immediate success—25,000 download the app within 24 hours.

January 2011: Instagram hits 1 million users.

February 2011: Instagram introduces hashtags and releases API to developers; Systrom raises another $7 million in investment funds.

July 2011: Jessica Zollman is hired as Instagram's first community evangelist; more than 100 million pictures have been uploaded to Instagram.

January 2012: Krieger attends the State of the Union address as First Lady Michelle Obama's guest.

April 2012: Sequoia Capital invests $50 million in Instagram.

April 2, 2012: Instagram launches an Android version of the app—it's downloaded more than 1 million times in the first day.

April 4, 2012: Systrom turns down Twitter's $500 million offer to buy Instagram.

April 6, 2012: Systrom meets with Mark Zuckerberg about a possible Instagram-Facebook deal.

April 9, 2012: Facebook announces its plans to acquire Instagram for $1 billion in cash and stock.

May 18, 2012: Facebook becomes a publically traded company.

September 2012: Instagram closes the deal with Facebook; the team moves to Facebook's Menlo Park, California, offices.

December 17, 2012: Changes in the terms of services spark controversy over advertisers possibly using user information and photos.

March 2013: Emily White is hired as director of business operations at Instagram.

April 2013: Systrom is included on the *Time* 100 most influential list.

June 2013: Instagram launches a video feature—the app reaches more than 100 million users.

September 2013: Instagram has brought its total number of employees up to fifty.

November 1, 2013: Instagram adds ads for the first time.

January 2014: Instagram Direct allows users to send photos and videos to specific users; Instagram app is released for the Windows Phone.

Glossary

acquisition Something, such as a company, that is bought or otherwise obtained.

annotate To add notes or comments to a piece of writing or picture.

browser A software application that's used to find and display websites, such as Yahoo! and Google.

common stock Shares of a company, which permit a shareholder to money that the company makes.

entrepreneur A person who starts a business and takes on the risks involved in order to earn a profit.

exposure The act of subjecting sensitive material, such as camera film, to light.

fellow Someone, usually a student, given money or time to pursue research or special academic study.

fraternity An organization of U.S. college students that are commonly all male.

interface The system that controls how data or information is shown on a computer and the way a user works with the computer.

invest To provide up-front funding to a company or business in order to make a profit in return.

lucrative Able to produce a lot of money.

microblogging Writing short, online posts on a weblog, or blog.

minutiae Small, often mundane, details.

net worth The value of all assets a person or company has.

nostalgia An emotion of both happiness and sadness in remembering something from the past that a person might want to experience again.

notoriety The state of being generally known.

saturation The fullness or intensity of the colors in a photograph, which can be increased or decreased in photo-editing software.

paparazzi Photographers that follow famous people in order to photograph them and sell the photographs.

podcast A radio-like program that may include music, talk, or both, available on the Internet.

proficiency The quality of being good at something or having expertise.

prolific The state of being very productive or abundant.

promotion The act of furthering the growth of something, especially sales or publicity.

prototype The first version of something on which other later models are based.

restricted stock Shares of a company that cannot be passed to another person unless certain conditions are met.

revenue The money made from a business or investment.

seed money The money used to help start a project or company.

software The set of programs used on a computer or mobile device.

spam Annoying messages sent to many people over the Internet.

stock market The marketplace in which the shares of companies are sold.

style sheet A text file that includes the font and layout formatting for a website.

tabloid Media, including magazines, newspapers, and TV shows, that features photographs, especially of celebrities, and short accompanying stories.

terms of service The rules to which a user must agree in order to use a website, app, or other product.

theoretical Having to do with a theory, or the general rules or ideas governing a subject.

thesis A very long paper written on a specific topic completed to earn a college degree.

visa An official mark or stamp on a passport that allows the bearer to enter or leave a country.

For More Information

Canadian Youth Business Foundation (CYBF)
133 Richmond Street West, Suite 700
Toronto, ON M5H 2L3
Canada
(866) 646-2922
Website: http://www.cybf.ca
Young adults can find advice on starting a business at the
   Canadian Youth Business Foundation. From financing
   to mentoring and networking, the foundation helps
   bring startups to life.

Family Online Safety Institute (FOSI)
400 7th Street NW, Suite 306
Washington, DC 20004
(202) 775-0158
Website: http://www.fosi.org
The Family Online Safety Institute works around the
   world with governments and those in the tech
   industry to protect Internet users. It puts on
   events and supplies information about online
   safety as well.

iD Tech Camps
910 East Hamilton Aveue, Suite 300
Campbell, CA 95008
(888) 709-8324
Website: http://www.idtech.com
iD Tech Camps run computer and technology camps
  for teens at locations across the Unites States.

Immigrant Learning Center
442 Main Street
Malden, MA 02148
(781) 321-1963
Website: http://www.ilctr.org
The Immigrant Learning Center helps immigrants
  in Massachusetts learn English and develop
  skills to further their careers in the United
  States.

Mayfield Fellows Program
Stanford Technology Ventures Program
Stanford University
Huang Engineering Center
475 Via Ortega, Suite 003
Stanford, CA 94305
(650) 723-2164
Website: http://stvp.stanford.edu/teaching/mfp

The Mayfield Fellows Program connects Stanford University students with mentors in the technology field. Students take classes and do an internship to learn more about entrepreneurship, leadership, and the business of a startup company.

National Venture Capital Association (NVCA)
1655 Fort Myer Drive, Suite 850
Arlington, VA 22209
(703) 524-2549
Website: http://www.nvca.org
One of the foremost trade organizations for startup investors, the NVCA supplies data for its members and works to support policies that will aid entrepreneurs and venture capitalists into the future.

Startup Canada
50 O'Connor Street, Suite 300
Ottawa, ON K1P 6L2
Canada
(613) 316-6203
Website: http://www.startupcan.ca
Those looking to learn more about starting a company can take part in Startup Canada. It helps entrepreneurs in Canada network, learn leadership skills,

and work with the government and communities around the country to foster a good environment for startups.

SXSW Interactive
SXSW, LLC
P.O. Box 685289
Austin, TX 78768
(512) 467-7979
Website: http://sxsw.com/interactive
The SXSW (South by Southwest) Interactive Festival takes place in Austin, Texas, each spring to showcase new technology. Presentations and panel discussions including some of the biggest names in the tech world are a big draw for entrepreneurs and new web developers looking for information and connections.

U.S. Internet Industry Association (USIIA)
P.O. Box 302
Luray, VA 22834
(540) 742-1928
Website: http://usiia-net.org
The USIIA works to support Internet business by supplying information to its members and promoting laws and policies that aid online commerce.

U.S. Securities and Exchange Commission (SEC)
100 F Street NE
Washington, DC 20549
(202) 942-8088
Website: http://www.sec.gov
The Securities and Exchange Commission regulates business practices in the United States. It works to protect investors and their investments.

WEBSITES

Because of the changing nature of Internet links, Rosen Publishing has developed an online list of Web sites related to the subject of this book. This site is updated regularly. Please use this link to access the list:

http://www.rosenlinks.com/IBIO/Inst

For Further Reading

Beahm, George, ed. *The Billionaire Boy: Mark Zuckerberg in His Own Words.* Chicago, IL: B2 Books, 2012.

Bernstein, Ben. *A Teen's Guide to Success: How to Be Calm, Confident, Focused.* Huntsville, UT: Familius, 2013.

Blumenthal, Karen. *Steve Jobs: The Man Who Thought Different.* New York, NY: Feiwel and Friends, 2012.

Bonnice, Sherry. *Computer Programmer.* Broomall, PA: Mason Crest, 2014.

Boyd, Danah. *It's Complicated: The Social Lives of Networked Teens.* New Haven, CT: Yale University Press, 2014.

Christen, Carol. *What Color Is Your Parachute? For Teens: Discovering Yourself, Defining Your Future.* Berkeley, CA: Ten Speed Press, 2010.

Donovan, Sandra. *Communication Smarts: How to Express Yourself Best in Conversations, Texts, E-mails, and More.* Minneapolis, MN: Twenty-First Century Books, 2013.

Edge, Christopher. *How to Make Money.* London, England: Scholastic, 2012.

Espejo, Roman, ed. *Location-Based Social Networking and Services.* Detroit, MI: Greenhaven Press, 2014.

Ford, Jerry Lee, Jr. *HTML, XHTML, and CSS for the Absolute Beginner.* Boston, MA: Course Technology/ Cengage Learning, 2010.

Gelber, Alexis, and Stephen Koepp, eds. *Fortune Zoom!* New York, NY: Time Home Entertainment, 2013.

Harris, Ashley Rae. *Facebook: The Company and Its Founders.* Minneapolis, MN: ABDO Publishing, 2013.

Head, Honor. *How to Handle Cyberbullying.* Mankato, MN: Smart Apple Media, 2015.

Hobbs, Mike. *Gadgets and Inventions.* Mankato, MN: Smart Apple Media, 2014.

James, Jack. *How to Let Your Parents Raise a Millionaire: A Kid-to-Kid View on How to Make Money, Make a Difference and Have Fun Doing Both.* New York, NY: Morgan James Publishing, 2012.

Larson, Elsie. *A Beautiful Mess Photo Idea Book: 95 Inspiring Ideas for Photographing Your Friends, Your World, and Yourself.* New York, NY: Amphoto Books, 2013.

Lusted, Marcia. *Apple: The Company and Its Visionary Founder, Steve Jobs.* Minneapolis, MN: ABDO Publishing, 2012.

Mara, Wil. *American Entrepreneurship.* New York, NY: Children's Press, 2014.

Patchin, Justin W., and Sameer Hinduja. *Words Wound: Delete Cyberbullying and Make Kindness Go Viral.* Minneapolis, MN: Free Spirit Publishing, 2013.

Qualman, Erik. *What Happens in Vegas Stays on YouTube.* Cambridge, MA: Equalman Studios, 2014.

Rankin, Kenrya. *Start It Up: The Complete Teen Business Guide to Turning Your Passions into Pay.* San Francisco, CA: Zest Books, 2011.

Riggs, Jason R. *Python for Kids: A Playful Introduction to Programming.* San Francisco, CA: No Starch Press, 2012.

Stone, Brad. *The Everything Store: Jeff Bezos and the Age of Amazon.* New York, NY: Little, Brown and Company, 2013.

This Is Happening: Life Through the Lens of Instagram. San Francisco, CA: Chronicle Books, 2013.

Vaynerchuk, Gary. *Jab, Jab, Jab, Right Hook: How to Tell Your Story in a Noisy, Social World.* New York, NY: Harper Business, 2013.

Bibliography

Bertoni, Steven. "Instagram's Kevin Systrom: The Stanford Billionaire Machine Strikes Again." *Forbes*, August 20, 2012. Retrieved February 27, 2014 (http://www.forbes.com/sites/stevenbertoni/2012/08/01/instagrams-kevin-systrom-the-stanford-millionaire-machine-strikes-again).

Carlson, Nicholas. "Industry People Are Whispering That Kevin Systrom Blew It Selling Instagram for $1 Billion." *Business Insider*, November 14, 2013. Retrieved February 25, 2014 (http://www.businessinsider.com/industry-people-are-whispering-that-kevin-systrom-blew-it-selling-instagram-for-1-billion-2013-11#ixzz2uHLIRdH9).

Carr, Austin. "How Instagram CEO Kevin Systrom Is Making Good on Facebook's Billion Dollar Bet." *Fast Company*, July/August 2013. Retrieved February 25, 2014 (http://www.fastcompany.com/3012565/how-instagram-ceo-kevin-systrom-is-making-good-on-facebooks-billion-dollar-bet).

Constine, Josh. "Instagram Cofounder Mike Krieger's 8 Principles for Building Products People Want." TechCrunch.com, November 30, 2012. Retrieved February 26, 2014 (http://techcrunch.com/2012/11/30/instagram-cofounder-mike-kriegers-8-principles-for-building-products-people-want).

Gottems, Leonardo. "Meet the Brazilian Behind Instagram." Intelligenthq.com, April 4, 2012. Retrieved February 28, 2014 (http://www.intelligenthq.com/technology/ meet-the-brazilian-behind-instagram).

Guynn, Jessica. "How Instagram Founder Kevin Systrom Became Insta-Rich." *Los Angeles Times*, April 11, 2012. Retrieved March 9, 2014 (http://articles.latimes .com/print/2012/apr/11/business/la-fi-instagram -systrom-20120411).

Hamburger, Ellis. "Sketching Instagram: Cofounder Mike Krieger Reveals the Photo App's Humble Beginnings." TheVerge.com, May 13, 2013. Retrieved February 28, 2014 (http://www.theverge.com/2013/5/13/4296760/ sketching-instagram-cofounder-mike-krieger -reveals-apps-humble-beginnings).

Handler, Mitchell. "Instagram Founders Offer Stories, Advice on Campus." *Daily Cal*, September 10, 2013. Retrieved February 26, 2014 (http://www.dailycal.org/ 2013/09/10/instagram-founders-offer-stories-advice -on-campus).

Krieger, Mike. "Celebrating Startups in the State of the Union." White House Blog, January 31, 2012. Retrieved February 28, 2014 (http://www .whitehouse.gov/blog/2012/01/31/celebrating -startups-state-union).

Lagorio-Chafkin, Christine. "Kevin Systrom and Mike Krieger, Founders of Instagram." *Inc.*, April 9, 2012.

Retrieved February 25, 2014 (http://www.inc.com/ 30under30/2011/profile-kevin-systrom-mike-krieger -founders-instagram.html).

Louis, Tristan. "How Much Do Average Apps Make?" *Forbes*, August 10, 2013. Retrieved March 11, 2014 (http://www .forbes.com/sites/tristanlouis/2013/08/10/how-much -do-average-apps-make).

Madden Mary, et al. "Teens, Social Media, and Privacy." Pew Research Center Internet Project, May 21, 2013. Retrieved March 6, 2014 (http://www.pewinternet.org/ 2013/05/21/teens-social-media-and-privacy).

Marston, Rebecca. "Instagram's Founders Kevin Systrom and Mike Krieger." BBC News, April 10, 2012. Retrieved February 25, 2014 (http://www.bbc.com/news/ business-17661976).

Middlesex "Middlesex Connections." Fall 2011. Retrieved March 4, 2014 (https://www.mxschool .edu/sites/default/files/uploads/mdsx-bulletin%20 fa11%20web.pdf).

Mundkur, Yatin. "Immigrant Entrepreneurs: Vital for American Innovation." *Forbes* Techonomy Blog, January 23, 2014. Retrieved March 9, 2014 (http:// www.forbes.com/sites/techonomy/2014/01/23/ immigrant-entrepreneurs-vital-for-american -innovation).

Patel, Nilay. "No, Instagram Can't Sell Your Photos: What the New Terms of Service Really Mean." TheVerge.com,

December 18, 2012. Retrieved February 25, 2014 (http://www.theverge.com/2012/12/18/3780158/instagrams-new-terms-of-service-what-they-really-mean).

Quora. "Kevin Systrom, CEO at Instagram." Retrieved February 26, 2014 (http://www.quora.com/Kevin-Systrom/answers).

Raice, Shayndi, and Spencer E. Ante. "Insta-Rich: $1 Billion for Instagram." *Wall Street Journal*, April 10, 2012. Retrieved February 25, 2014 (http://online.wsj.com/news/articles/SB10001424052702303815404577333840377381670).

Ritchie, Rene. "History of iPhone: From Revolution to What Comes Next." Imore.com, September 9, 2013. Retrieved March 1, 2014 (http://www.imore.com/history-iphone).

Rusli, Evelyn M. "Instagram Pictures Itself Making Money." *Wall Street Journal*, September 8, 2013. Retrieved February 25, 2014 (http://online.wsj.com/news/articles/SB1000142412788732457730457905923069305894).

Seacrest, Ryan. "Kevin Systrom." *Time*, April 18, 2013. Retrieved March 6, 2014 (http://time100.time.com/2013/04/18/time-100/slide/kevin-systrom).

Sengupta, Somini, Nicole Perlroth, and Jenna Wortham. "Behind Instagram's Success, Networking the Old Way." *New York Times*, April 13, 2012. Retrieved February 27, 2014 (http://www.nytimes.com/2012/04/14/technology/

instagram-founders-were-helped-by-bay-area
-connections.html?pagewanted=all&_r=2&).

Setup Interview. "Mike Krieger, Cofounder of Instagram."
November 4, 2011. Retrieved February 26, 2014 (http://
mike.krieger.usesthis.com).

Siegler, M.G. "Distilled from Burbn, Instagram Makes Quick
Beautiful Photos Social (Preview)." TechCrunch.com,
September 20, 2010. Retrieved March 10, 2014 (http://
techcrunch.com/2010/09/20/instagram).

Swisher, Kara. "The Money Shot." *Vanity Fair*, June 2013.
Retrieved February 25, 2014 (http://www.vanityfair
.com/business/2013/06/kara-swisher-instagram).

Thompson, Clive. "Clive Thompson on the Instagram
Effect." *Wired*, January 2012. Retrieved February 25,
2014 (http://www.wired.com/magazine/2011/12/
st_thompson_instagram).

Weber, Tim. "Facebook's Instagram Deal: Can One App
Be Worth $1bn?" *BBC News*, April 10, 2013. Retrieved
February 25, 2014 (http://www.bbc.com/news/
business-17666032).

Index

ABOUT THE AUTHOR

Kristen Rajczak studied English and journalism at Gannon University in Erie, Pennsylvania, and received her master's degree in arts journalism at the S. I. Newhouse School of Public Communications at Syracuse University. She blogged and tweeted through her graduate school experience, also dabbling in Flash, Photoshop, HTML, and CSS, and came out the other side with a great appreciation for the changing media landscape brought about by social networking and the web. Today, Rajczak is a children's book editor and writer. She lives in Buffalo, New York.

PHOTO CREDITS